The Mountain was the goal, the journey was the lesson

Hiking Mount
THIELSEN

ANDREW M BENAGE

Published by Hemingway Publishers

Cover design by Hemingway Publishers

ISBN: Printed in the United States

TABLE OF CONTENTS

DEDICATION

To my family and friends who always support me in every goal I chase. To my wife, Tiffany — my biggest supporter and constant encourager — thank you for believing in me through every crazy idea, from hiking remote mountains to keeping bees to giving up birthday weekends so I can race my bike. Your love and support mean everything.

And to my Heavenly Father, who inspired both the climb and this book — I'm grateful for a Father in Heaven who guides me to grow in all aspects of life and provides the means to do so.

ACKNOWLEDGEMENT

I want to begin by thanking my wife, Tiffany. She was not only my biggest supporter but also my sounding board through every stage of this process. She listened to me read this book more times than I can count, helped me sort through my thoughts, and encouraged me to keep going even when I doubted myself. Her patience, insight, and love made this book possible in more ways than one.

I'd also like to thank the team at Hemingway Publishers for their guidance and expertise. They helped turn my rough collection of words and ideas into something far better than I could have imagined, smoothing out all my spelling and grammatical errors along the way.

Much of the inspiration for this book came from my love of the outdoors — from discovering new trails and remote places that remind me how small we are compared to the world around us, yet how personal and intentional God's creations truly are.

Finally, I want to express my gratitude to my Heavenly Father. In our home, goal setting has always been guided by principles taught through the Church of Jesus Christ of Latter Day Saints — setting spiritual, physical, social, and intellectual goals to grow and improve in every area of life. That process not only inspired this hike but also gave me the courage and direction to write about it. I'm thankful for a Father in Heaven who wants me to grow and provides the inspiration and strength to do it.

ABOUT THE AUTHOR

Andrew Benage is from Stanfield, Oregon, though he grew up in several areas across the Pacific Northwest. He lives with his wife, Tiffany, and their two children, Braxton and Stella, on a small "hobby farm" with goats, chickens, turkeys, bees, and a garden.

Andrew's love for exploring the outdoors began in his youth as a Boy Scout, where he spent countless hours hiking, camping, and learning survival skills. That passion was further shaped by his two years in Alaska on a mission for the Church of Jesus Christ of Latter-Day Saints, where he hiked, fished, and experienced remote wilderness. Today, that love continues as a family activity — he and his family enjoy taking hikes together, exploring new trails, and sharing adventures.

By profession, Andrew is a sales representative for an industrial hose and fitting supply company. Years of working in sales have taught him the value of perseverance, planning, and following through — lessons he applies not just in work, but in his personal pursuits.

Andrew enjoys hiking, camping, hunting, cycling, and beekeeping, especially when it means discovering new places. He also enjoys watching soccer. The inspiration to hike Mount Thielsen led him to write this book, reflecting on the connection between challenging physical goals and personal growth in life.

A devoted member of his faith, Andrew believes that life is meant to help us grow — spiritually, mentally, and physically — and that our experiences are opportunities to become closer to our Heavenly Father and to work toward becoming like Him.

INTRO

Many people know, either from experiencing it themselves or from seeing pictures, that the state of Oregon is full of beautiful natural scenery. For work, I get the unique opportunity to travel to different parts of Oregon on a weekly basis, and at different times of the year. This has given me the chance to see many captivating views, often in completely different seasons.

One of the drives I make regularly is on Highway 97, which runs north and south through the entire state, along the east side of the Cascade Mountain Range. This highway offers some amazing views of the various peaks in that range.

One day, on my way home, I had to take a slightly different route than usual. As I was almost back to the highway I normally travel on, I turned a corner, and suddenly saw a completely different view of the terrain and noticed a mountain I hadn't really noticed before.

It stood tall and striking above miles of deep green pine trees. The peak reminded me instantly of the famous Matterhorn, maybe not as grand, but definitely unique and beautiful in its own way. The top was still mostly covered in snow, but you could see the rocky terrain stretching upward into the sky.

I can't really explain why, but the moment I saw it, I felt this strong desire to hike it. I didn't know anything about the mountain, not even its name, or whether it was something people actually climbed. But something about it just called me. Later, I found out that the mountain was Mount Thielsen, part of the Cascade Range in southern Oregon.

Around that same time, my family and I had been working on setting personal goals for the year, for the things we wanted to improve or experiences we wanted to have across different parts of life. We had been talking about setting goals in four areas of our lives: Spiritual, Social, Physical, and Intellectual.

That framework really helped me focus, and as I started thinking about my goals and researching the mountain, an idea started to take shape: I wanted to hike it. And not only that, I wanted to write a book about the experience.

There was something about the timing that felt meaningful. The idea of challenging myself physically, while also reflecting upon the personal growth in different parts of my life, is all tied together. Somehow, the mountain became more than just a place I wanted to visit. It became a symbol of what it means to set goals, push yourself, and grow.

This book is about that journey; both the hike itself and everything it represents. It's about the connection between the trail and the goals we set in life. It's a personal story, but one I hope others can relate to, whether you're setting big goals, climbing literal mountains, or just trying to move forward in your own way.

My love for the outdoors didn't start with Mount Thielsen. It goes back to my childhood in Boy Scouts, where I learned to camp, hike, and navigate the wilderness. Those early experiences taught me more than just outdoor skills; they taught me patience, perseverance, and the value of planning ahead.

Later, I spent two years in Alaska on a mission for my church. Exploring glaciers, fishing in remote streams, and hiking through untouched wilderness gave me an even deeper appreciation for the raw beauty and challenges nature can offer. Those experiences shaped not just my physical endurance, but also my perspective on tackling goals, whether in the woods or in life.

During that time, I learned the real power of setting goals. Every day we planned what we hoped to accomplish—from small, simple tasks to ambitious goals that stretched us spiritually and mentally. We planned as companions, as zones, and even as an entire mission. There was a lot of planning, but through it, I learned consistency and purpose. I still remember one day when my companion and I set what seemed like a silly goal: to see a moose. Moose were everywhere in Alaska, but we hadn't seen one in several days, and our motivation was running low. So we added it to our list—"see one moose." That day, sure enough, we did. It might sound like a coincidence, but for me, it became a quiet reminder that God is aware of us, even in the smallest things. He wants us to grow and succeed, and when we set our sights on something—no matter how simple—He will help guide us toward it.

Today, the outdoors remains a family affair. We camp, hike, and explore together, making memories while challenging ourselves physically and mentally. Our family also uses this time to reflect on personal goals. Halfway through each year, we check in with each other to see how we're doing with the goals we set. This accountability keeps us motivated and connected. It's one thing to set a goal for yourself, but sharing it with people you care about adds purpose and perspective.

Oregon is full of remarkable places that many people have never seen. Beyond the well-known peaks and trails, there are hidden wonders like Fort Rock, Crack in the Ground, and the Paisley Caves. Traveling for work has given me the privilege of glimpsing these remote corners of the state. That exposure has taught me to notice the unexpected, to find beauty where others might pass by, and to stay curious. It's that same mindset I brought to Mount Thielsen, open to the unknown, ready for adventure, and eager to see what lies around the next corner.

CHAPTER 1

CHOOSING YOUR MOUNTAIN, CLARIFYING GOALS

Driving home that day, I didn't have the intention of finding a mountain I wanted to hike. But when I saw it, something inside me lit up. A desire I hadn't expected hit me all at once: I want to hike that!

Sometimes our goals are like that. We aren't actively looking for them, but then something triggers a thought or feeling inside us, and suddenly we think, I want to do that. It might be something we don't currently do, or something we've never even considered, but the spark is there.

And often, we don't know what the journey will require. When I decided I wanted to hike Mount Thielsen, I knew almost nothing about it. I didn't know if it was even possible to hike. If it was, how long was the trail? Was it an overnight trip or a day hike? How steep would it be? I had no answers, just a desire, and sometimes, that's all it takes to get started.

The same goes for our personal goals. We rarely have all the answers at the beginning, but the important thing is being willing to start. And often, starting simply means doing a little research.

When I began looking into Mount Thielsen, I quickly learned it wasn't going to be an easy hike. The trail to the summit was only five miles, but it climbed nearly 3,800 feet in that short distance. That meant I needed to prepare, physically and mentally, before I could take it on. (We'll get into the preparation side in the next chapter.)

But here's something I realized early on: don't let the research scare you off.

In reading about the hike, certain words kept popping up: technical, scramble, steep, spire, exposure, and lightning rod. Not exactly comforting! It was described as dangerous, difficult, and even crowded. But every now and then, one word would appear that kept me hooked: stunning.

That one word: stunning… kept me coming back.

When it comes to goals, we sometimes let the challenges stop us before we even begin. We hear a few hard truths about how tough it'll be, and we decide it's not worth it. Human nature tends to lean toward comfort, toward the path of least resistance. But the problem is, there's no growth on that path.

Setting clear, realistic goals can help bring that spark of inspiration into focus.

I remember when my wife, Tiffany, set a goal to learn how to use her Cricut machine. At first, her goal was simple: learn how to use it. But I suggested she adjust it slightly, to focus not on mastering the whole thing, but on becoming more proficient with it. That small shift gave the goal some breathing room.

The difference may sound minor, but it was huge. If her goal had stayed rigid, she would have felt pressure to master every function, every technique, and every project idea. And six months later, if she hadn't done all of that, it could have left her discouraged... like she'd failed. But by aiming for "more proficient," every small step counted. If she learned a couple of new features, tried a different project, or gained confidence in one area, she could celebrate that progress.

And that's what happened. Instead of being weighed down by the pressure of "mastery," she had room to grow at her own pace. Every new thing she learned added to her sense of accomplishment, rather than subtracting from it.

That lesson applies to so many of our goals. When we set the bar at perfection, we're almost guaranteeing disappointment. If the only definition of success is "mastery," then anything less feels like failure. But when we frame our goals with progress in mind, getting better, moving forward, becoming more consistent, we allow ourselves to grow.

I've noticed that perfection has a way of freezing people in place. I've met so many talented, capable people who never begin something simply because they're afraid they won't do it perfectly. They'll say things like, "I'll start when I have more time," or "I just need to learn a little more before I try." But weeks turn into months, and months into years, and that mountain stays in the distance. The truth is, starting messy is better than waiting for perfect conditions that never come.

Growth only happens in motion. When you take one small, imperfect step toward a goal, you learn something you couldn't have learned by standing still. And those lessons, both the successes and the missteps, become the very things that shape you for the next climb.

It's the difference between saying, "I want to get in shape" and "I want to consistently exercise three times a week." Or between "I want to save $20,000 this year" and "I want to consistently set aside 10% of every paycheck." The first versions are mountains that feel overwhelming. The second version breaks the climb into manageable steps.

Choosing your mountain isn't just about what inspires you; it's also about setting yourself up to keep climbing. If the mountain you choose feels impossible from the beginning, you're far more likely to quit. But if you choose a mountain that challenges you and gives you room to grow, you'll be much more likely to stay on the trail long enough to reach the top.

Even small steps are real progress. And that progress matters.

One habit that often helps people is writing down their goals, no matter how small they seem. There's something powerful about putting words on paper; it takes an idea out of your head and gives it shape. You can jot down goals on sticky notes and place them on your bathroom mirror or dashboard. Seeing them every day reminds us of what we are aiming for. Some days we'll take a big step forward; other days, it's just a tiny one. But each checkmark builds momentum.

The funny thing is that the act of tracking progress becomes its own motivation. Even when I didn't feel like it, I could look back and see the trail behind me. That visible reminder... "Look how far you've already come" ... can be the difference between giving up and pushing on.

At work, this principle plays out for me every year. As a sales rep with a defined territory, my job depends on consistent growth, and growth never happens by accident. At the beginning of each year, I sit down and map out what I want that growth to look like. I break it down month by month, setting realistic targets that add up to a clear total by year's end. Once those numbers are written down, they're no longer vague ideas floating around in my head; they're measurable goals that I can see and track.

Each month, I check my progress and compare it to where I planned to be. Sometimes I'm ahead, sometimes I'm a little behind, but either way, it keeps me accountable. Having that plan in writing gives me a sense of direction and focus. It helps me adjust when needed and celebrate small wins along the way. I've learned that when a goal is written and reviewed often, it becomes a living thing; it stays in front of mind, and that awareness alone helps drive action. The same is true for personal goals. When we put them in writing and look at them regularly, we remind ourselves not just what we're chasing, but why we started climbing in the first place.

Another example of setting clear goals comes from something I've struggled with personally, and that is reading.

I've never been big into reading. I like the idea of reading a lot of books, but I've always had a hard time actually making the conscious decision to sit down and do it. About a year ago, I decided I wanted to get better at it.

Now, a goal like "read more books" sounds fine on the surface, but it's really broad. What does "more" mean? If I read one book all year, technically that's more than I usually read. So, I had to get more specific.

I set a clearer goal: I want to read four books this year.

I know for most people, that number might sound small, but for me, that was a new mountain. It was something I'd never done before, and it felt challenging but doable. With that number in mind, and eventually written down, I started working toward it.

And sure enough, I did it. I finished my fourth book by the end of November, and with some momentum built up, I picked up one more and finished my fifth book before the year ended.

All of that happened because the goal was clear. I knew what I was aiming for. That simple clarity made all the difference.

Looking back, I realized that motivation is fragile when it has no target. When you give your effort a name, a number, or a finish line, it suddenly becomes real. You start to feel accountable, not to anyone else, but to yourself. That's what the four-book goal did for me. It gave me structure without making me feel boxed in. I could choose what to read, how fast, and when, but I still had a direction.

There were days when I didn't feel like reading at all. But because the goal was clear, I could remind myself, "This chapter gets me closer." And that was enough to keep turning pages.

That's the thing with big or intimidating goals; they feel more manageable when we break them down. If you've got a mountain staring back at you, zoom out. Look at the overall goal, then figure out a few clear steps that will move you in that direction.

Instead of being overwhelmed, give yourself clarity. Clear goals give you traction.

But what about when we don't have a mountain calling us? What if we're just trying to figure out what goals we even want to set?

Unfortunately, some of the clearest goals in life come from the hardest moments.

I have a good friend who has struggled with his weight most of his life. What I didn't realize until recently was how deeply it affected him, not just physically, but also mentally and emotionally. A few years ago, we started working out regularly together. I assumed he was just trying to get in better shape.

But later, he opened up and told me it was about more than just losing weight. He had been dealing with depression. He described coming home from work, sitting on the couch, and not really engaging with his family. He admitted he just didn't care anymore.

Eventually, that mindset cost him more than he expected; he went through a divorce and saw his relationship with his kids start to suffer. That was his low point. But it was also the moment he realized something needed to change. That's when he found his mountain.

Since then, he's made huge strides, not just in his physical health, but in his attitude, his energy, and his connection with his kids. He even told me recently about the ripple effect: getting promoted at work, feeling more capable, and wanting to keep improving in every area of life.

The point is, sometimes goals are born out of inspiration. Other times, they come from desperation.

But either way, they matter.

And often, those goals that come from the hardest moments and the lowest valleys end up being the most meaningful. Because when everything feels unclear, sometimes that's when we finally see the mountain we need to climb.

And we realize… we actually want to.

I think God sometimes lets us sit in the valley long enough to recognize how badly we need to climb. The stillness, the discouragement, the discomfort; they're not punishments; they're invitations. When life feels quiet or hard, it's often because we're being shown a new summit to pursue.

Every mountain begins with a moment like that first glimpse I had of Mount Thielsen, something inside of us whispering, That's the one. The challenge isn't just to notice the mountain; it's to take the first step toward it. Whether your mountain is physical, spiritual, or deeply personal, the same truth holds: the climb will change you more than the view ever could.

CHAPTER 2

PREPARING THE PACK, PLANNING AND PREPARATION

As I mentioned before, I quickly realized that this wasn't going to be an easy hike. This wasn't the kind of trail you could just show up to and tackle on a whim. Mount Thielsen demanded preparation, both physical and mental.

It even has a nickname for a reason: the "Lightning Rod of the Cascades." The peak is remote, bare of trees, and steep, conditions that make it a magnet for lightning. In fact, it's been struck more than any other mountain in the Cascade Range.

Learning this also made me understand why: the Southern Oregon Cascades act as a natural funnel for moisture from the west and south. When that moist air meets the warm desert air in the afternoon, thunderstorms can appear almost out of nowhere. That meant timing my hike became a key part of my preparation. There was even one year I had to cancel because the forecast showed a storm moving in, right over the mountain.

The steepness of the trail was another challenge. Like I mentioned earlier, the mountain climbs nearly 3,800 feet in just five miles, a workout for muscles I hadn't been using regularly. I needed to build up my cardio and strengthen my legs so my body could handle the climb.

The mental preparation was a little easier. If I set my mind to something, I usually follow through. We often remind our kids that the brain is an incredibly powerful organ. There's real science behind that, too. The placebo effect shows how belief can change outcomes, athletes who mentally rehearse plays perform better in games, and patients with positive outlooks recover faster after surgery.

So, before I even started the hike, I told myself, "You CAN do this."

Then came packing my backpack. Mount Thielsen is remote. The nearest town is about a thirty-minute drive, and the fastest emergency response on the trail could take one to two hours. I needed to be ready for the unexpected: first aid, extra water, layers for changing weather, gear in case of an overnight stay, and protection for wildlife encounters.

Most of these items I never touched during the hike. But having them ready gave me confidence.

When an afternoon storm threatened the day of the climb, I left extremely early, while it was still dark. There's something about heading out into the woods an hour and a half before sunrise, by yourself, that really adds to the mental challenge. The forest is alive with sounds, and when you can't see more than ten or fifteen feet ahead, it can feel… well, a little unnerving.

A few times, I thought to myself, maybe I should just turn back and wait for daylight. But every time that thought crept in,

I remembered the looming storm. I took a deep breath, kept moving, and told myself, 'Step by step, the light will come.'

That, I think, is exactly what mental challenges feel like when pursuing a goal. Usually, when we start something new, we're stepping out into the dark. We know where we want to end up, but the first steps are uncertain.

I see that same lesson unfolding with my daughter, Stella. She tends to struggle with the unknown sometimes. When she sets a goal, her mind immediately races to the how—how will this work, what will I say, what if it doesn't go right? Recently, our family was asked to speak in church in a neighboring town. The moment we told her, her worries started pouring out: "What do I talk about? How many people will be there? I can't speak in front of everyone!" But as the evening went on, and she took time to think, pray, and listen, something shifted. She found a topic she felt inspired to share. She let her mom and me help her prepare, and little by little, her confidence grew. That unknown that once felt overwhelming began to take shape. We've seen it in other moments, too—when she volunteers to sing solos at church or faces a new sports season, unsure of her team or coaches. Each time, she learns to step into the unknown with faith and courage, and every time, she grows a little more.

Just like Stella learning to step into new challenges, every journey—big or small—starts with those first uncertain steps. We're learning the ropes, whether it's healthy eating, weightlifting, or building endurance for cardio. That first mile might feel impossible. That first decision to choose the apple over the chocolate bar might feel insignificant. But every small step forward is part of finding your path.

Eventually, the light starts to break through. For me, the beginning of the trail ran north along the western side of the mountain and nearby hills. The sun rose partly behind the peak, and as I climbed out of the first section of trees, I began to catch glimpses of the mountain illuminated by the morning light. Every turn of the trail revealed a new view, each one a little brighter than the previous one.

This is exactly how progress works with goals. Once we move past that initial "in the dark" stage, we start to see glimpses of what we're working toward. Maybe it's adding more weight at the gym because the smaller weights no longer challenge you. Maybe it's finishing a mile run without stopping for breath. Maybe it's sticking to a small habit consistently until it finally feels natural.

Those little accomplishments are the perfect mental boosters. They illuminate our path, build confidence, and give us the energy to keep moving forward. Step by step, and goal by goal, light begins to show the way.

Packing my backpack also reminded me that we can "pack" for life goals, too. Just like I prepared gear for a potential overnight hike, I can prepare tools to help me reach my personal goals. One of my long-term goals has been learning Spanish. I've never been naturally good at languages, but I've always believed that language is a gift, and that's a gift I just wasn't blessed with. For a few years, I've been slowly learning basic Spanish, often doing five-minute lessons each day. Most of the time, it feels like I'm barely making any progress.

But just like packing the right items for a hike, I found ways to "pack" for my Spanish goal. I discovered an app that gives me daily progress, I found a book to immerse myself in stories, and I began practicing when ordering food or talking with Spanish speakers who know little or no English. Each tool I added to my "pack" gave me a small advantage and helped me keep moving forward.

Every now and then, I catch glimpses of the light. When I'm at a Mexican restaurant and can hold a slightly longer conversation with the patient waitress, that's a small victory. When coaching my kids' soccer team, and I can explain drills to a player in broken Spanish, that's another beam of light breaking through. Even when the city brought goats to a neighboring property and I could have a basic conversation with the caretaker, that's progress.

None of these moments are fluency, but they are past the pitch-black stage, where I had no idea how to complete the goal. These glimpses keep me on the path, just like the first glimpses of light on Mount Thielsen kept me moving forward, step by step.

Preparation isn't just about packing; it's about thinking through the process and setting yourself up to reach your goal.

But there's a balance. Overpacking can become its own challenge. My wife is the queen of overpacking. When we first got married, even a single overnight trip looked like a month-long expedition with her luggage. On the flip side, her careful preparation saved me countless times when I forgot the basics.

The same principle applies to goals. You can overthink and over-prepare, but too much can weigh you down. When I read all the words used to describe Mount Thielsen: steep, scramble, exposure, and technical, I could have easily gone overboard and packed for every possible scenario. That would have made the hike heavier and harder. Mentally, some of those warnings got to me. I questioned if I should postpone it, maybe even wait another year.

But in the end, I kept my eyes on the summit. I wanted that view at the end of the trail. And because I focused on preparation without overdoing it, I was able to set out with confidence and reach my goal.

And that's really what this hike, and most goals, come down to: preparation, balance, and persistence. You don't need to have every possible scenario figured out, but you do need to think ahead and make choices that set you up for success. Overdoing it can weigh you down, but under-preparing can leave you unready.

The key is knowing what matters most and focusing on that. Step by step, choice by choice, and preparation by preparation, you move closer to the summit of your own goals. And when you finally get there, when you reach that top, it's not just about the view or the accomplishment; it's about everything you learned along the way… about your resilience, your planning, and your ability to push forward even when it felt daunting.

Because every goal, like every mountain, feels intimidating at first. But with clarity, preparation, and a willingness to start, you realize something powerful: you actually can do it.

One of the hardest parts of preparing for Mount Thielsen was realizing that I didn't actually know what I was in for. Unlike hikes I'd done before, I couldn't picture the trail, the steepness, or how early I'd have to leave to beat a storm. Preparation, in this case, meant planning for uncertainty. I researched maps, read accounts from others who had completed the climb, and thought through potential scenarios, but the truth was, part of the challenge was embracing the unknown. Packing my bag wasn't just about items; it was about preparing my mind to adapt to whatever I would encounter on the trail.

This experience taught me an important lesson about flexibility. No matter how carefully you plan, the mountain, or any goal, will throw surprises at you. The storm forecast might change, fatigue might hit faster than expected, or terrain might be harder than the descriptions suggested. Preparation doesn't mean having every answer or eliminating every risk. It means giving yourself the tools, mindset, and adaptability to handle challenges as they come. Step by step, and decision by decision, you learn to balance caution with progress, and that balance makes the climb possible.

Preparing to hike Mount Thielsen wasn't just about packing the right gear; it was about building the strength and endurance my body would need. I added more focus to my morning workouts, especially my legs, and increased my cardio with longer bike rides. I also did smaller practice hikes, treating each one as a rehearsal for the big climb. Each practice hike was a test, not just of muscles, but of pacing, hydration, and mental endurance. Some days, I felt stronger than others. Some days, I realized how easily I could tire if I didn't fuel properly.

These small, deliberate steps weren't glamorous, but they were essential. The mountain didn't care if I was motivated; it only cared whether I was ready. And the more I trained, the more confident I felt that I could meet it step by step.

Preparation also meant being ready for the unexpected. In the first two years, I tried to climb Mount Thielsen, but circumstances beyond my control forced me to adjust my plans. One year, a massive storm rolled in right on the weekend I was scheduled to hike. The next year, wildfires closed the area entirely. Both times, I had to delay my climb and rethink my timing, but each setback taught me something valuable. I learned to plan for flexibility, to check weather and wildfire updates ahead of time, and to keep extra contingency in mind for my schedule. Those disappointments could have been discouraging, but instead, they became part of the preparation process. Just like life, goals don't always happen on the exact timetable we imagine. The lessons are in how we adapt, prepare, and keep moving toward the summit, even when the path changes unexpectedly.

CHAPTER 3

BREAKING CAMP, TAKING THE FIRST STEPS FORWARD

In the weeks leading up to the hike, I focused on strengthening my legs and building stamina. My usual workout routine got a little tweak: squats, lunges, and other leg exercises became a priority, and I added longer bike rides to improve cardio and endurance. At first, it felt like small progress; almost imperceptible, but each session gave me a bit more confidence that I could handle the climb. By the time I loaded up my truck for the hike, I wasn't just mentally prepared; I could feel my body ready, too. Those small, deliberate steps reminded me that preparation isn't just about planning; it's about consistent effort that compounds over time.

After years of mentally preparing and trying to build myself up physically, the day had finally arrived. I was ready to attempt the climb I'd dreamed about for so long. Originally, my wife was supposed to join me, but she came down sick the day before, leaving me to face the mountain alone. So, I packed up my gear, loaded the truck, and made the five-hour drive with both excitement and a little unease riding in the seat beside me.

I arrived at the campsite near the base of the mountain around 5 p.m. under dark skies. I had never been there before, so even finding a campsite felt like its own small adventure. Once

I decided on a campsite, I hurried to set up my tent and canopy. And then the storm hit.

The rain came hard, the kind that doesn't just fall but carves little rivers through the dirt. Lightning lit up the sky in blinding flashes, followed almost instantly by booming thunder. I cooked dinner under my canopy, laughing at the absurdity of it... me... a small figure under thin fabric, while one of the biggest storms I'd ever seen raged around me. As the storm danced over the nearby lake, I sat in awe, soaked in the sound and fury of it all.

When the rain finally eased, I crawled into my tent. To my relief, it was dry inside: a small victory. I lay there in the dark, lightning still occasionally splitting the night sky, and my thoughts began to spiral. Should I even attempt this hike tomorrow?

The doubts piled up quickly. There might be another storm the next afternoon. My hiking partner wasn't with me, and I knew the importance of having someone there in case things went wrong. The reasons to quit were stacking higher than the mountain itself.

Morning came early: 4 a.m. I packed up my wet tent, loaded my truck, and drove to the trailhead. But when I parked, the jitters came back. It was pitch black, so dark I couldn't even see the trailhead from my vehicle. A few other cars sat quietly with hikers asleep inside, waiting for the sunrise. And again, the excuses crept in: I don't want to wake up these people. I don't even know where the trail starts without a light. What if I ran into a bear?

But then I reminded myself of everything that had brought me here. I thought back to the first time I'd seen the mountain, standing proud on the horizon, sparking this goal in me. I remembered all the research I'd done to prepare. I thought about the gear I had packed carefully, every item chosen to keep me safe. And I remembered my frustration over the past couple of years when weather and wildfires had robbed me of this chance.

This wasn't my first attempt at Mount Thielsen. One year, a massive storm swept through the weekend I had planned to hike, forcing me to cancel. The next year, wildfires closed the area entirely. At times, I wondered if the universe was sending a message: maybe I wasn't meant to make it. But looking back, those setbacks were lessons in disguise. They taught me to pay attention to timing, weather, and unexpected obstacles. They reminded me that flexibility and patience are part of any meaningful goal. By the time I finally approached the trail, I felt not just anticipation, but preparedness for whatever could come my way.

Those reminders tipped the scale. I got out of the truck, put on my pack, switched on my headlamp, and started walking toward the trailhead.

One step, then another. The unknown began to fade as I moved forward.

And isn't that exactly how our goals feel? That first step is always the hardest. We feel it every January when New Year's resolutions roll around:

1. This year I'll start exercising.
2. I'll eat better.
3. I'll read more.
4. I'll be more present with my family.

But then January 1st arrives. We wake up tired from the night before and push our workout to "tomorrow." We tell ourselves we can't just throw away the leftover dessert, so we'll start eating better "after it's gone." We finish one book, but never pick up the next. We put down our phones to be more present with our kids, until the next bit of news or distraction pulls us back in.

Just like me sitting in that truck at the trailhead, we let excuses pile up until they bury the very goal we set out to accomplish.

So how do we take that first step? How do we push past the storm, the darkness, the uncertainty, and start our hike?

The truth is, there's no single answer that works for everyone. Life isn't that simple. Each of us carries different strengths and weaknesses. Some people thrive at goal setting; for others, the follow-through is the real challenge.

For me, the key has often been creating habits and keeping the end goal clearly in sight. I don't just set a goal to read books; I set it to build the habit of reading. I don't just practice Spanish to learn a few words; I do it so I can eventually hold real conversations. Most of my progress has come from keeping my eyes fixed on the "why" behind the goal.

Hiking Mount Thielsen solo added a different kind of challenge. I knew that if something went wrong, help could be hours away. That reality made me cautious, but it also made the journey intensely personal. I noticed details I might have overlooked with a partner: the sound of the wind in the trees, the way the first light hit the rocky peak, and the small milestones along the trail. At the same time, I missed sharing those moments with my wife, seeing her reaction, or trading stories along the way. But experiencing it alone forced me to rely on my own judgment, to celebrate small victories quietly, and to savor each step in a way that felt unique to me. It became a personal testament to the power of pushing forward, even when the support you usually rely on isn't right beside you.

That morning on the trail, as my eyes adjusted to the darkness and the horizon began to glow with the faint light of dawn, I felt the payoff of pushing through. Each bend in the trail revealed a new glimpse of the mountain, slowly illuminated. Those glimpses gave me energy to keep climbing, a reminder of what I was moving toward.

In the same way, small reminders of our goals can keep us going. Some people create vision boards, hanging them where they'll see them every day: a collage of the trip they want to take, the weight they want to lose, the skill they want to master. Those visuals are like the first rays of sun on the trail, giving clarity and encouragement just when we're tempted to turn back.

But visuals aren't the only tools we can use. Over the years, I've learned that finding the right tools can also make the difference between a goal that fizzles out and a goal that grows legs. For example, with my Spanish practice, the tool that has helped me the most is a simple app that tracks my daily practice streak. As of today, I've been on a streak of over 1,200 days. There are plenty of days when the thing that pushes me to open the app and practice, even if only for a few minutes, is the thought of not wanting to lose that streak. It's funny how a small number on a screen can become such a motivator.

The same has been true with reading. My goal to read four books a year suddenly became easier when I discovered an author whose writing style seemed tailor-made for me. His books flowed so smoothly that reading felt less like a chore and more like a reward. The tool in that case wasn't an app or a chart but simply finding the right kind of book, and letting enjoyment pull me forward.

But here's the caution: sometimes the tool can become the goal. With my Spanish app, I have to ask myself often: "Am I really practicing to learn and grow, or am I just protecting my streak number on my screen?" In those moments, the "streak" becomes hollow if I lose sight of the original "why" of the goal.

The same thing happened with another personal goal: quitting soda. For years, I had fallen into a bad habit of drinking what felt like a ridiculous amount of soda every day. I knew it wasn't healthy, so I decided to stop, and I did. For a long time, I felt great about it. My body felt better, my energy improved, and I was glad to be free of the bad habit. But years later, I caught myself wondering why I was still saying no to soda. Was it because I still felt strongly about the health benefits? Or was it just because I didn't want to break the streak?

Eventually, I realized I wasn't drinking soda anymore simply because of the number of years I had stacked up. I had lost sight of my original "why," and without it, the action felt empty.

And that's the real lesson: tools are valuable: apps, streaks, books, vision boards, and accountability partners, but they can only carry us so far. If we forget the deeper reason for our goal, the tool itself can trap us. A streak isn't growth. A stack of finished books isn't wisdom. The real power is remembering why we set out on the trail in the first place.

When we keep that "why" close, when we let it shine like the first rays of sunlight breaking over the horizon, it gives meaning to every step forward. And meaning is what will keep us climbing when the storm clouds gather, when the excuses pile up, and when the darkness feels too heavy.

CHAPTER 4

FIRST MILES THROUGH THE FOREST, BUILDING MOMENTUM

After the sun was up enough to see without my flashlight, I finally began to enjoy my surroundings more. I didn't have to focus solely on what was directly in front of me, dodging roots, rocks, or checking to see if I was still on the trail. I could look ahead, gauge the path, and get a better sense of where I was in the woods.

During this portion of the hike, I was still in the trees. Daylight was breaking through just as I emerged from the old burn scar that had kept me from attempting this hike the previous year. Looking back, I could see the damage the fire had caused: burned trees lying flat on the forest floor, craters marking where trees had been uprooted. It was sobering, yet fascinating, to see the contrast as I turned back toward the unscathed portions of the forest ahead.

From this vantage, I also caught sight of Diamond Lake. Even from this height, it looked vast. Just a few hours ago, I had been there packing up my wet gear, convincing myself to go through with the hike. Seeing how far I had already climbed reminded me that progress often comes in small, incremental steps, even if the finish line still feels far away.

At this point, I could start looking forward more as well. I could see the trees ahead, and I could gauge the angle of the trail, which, as my legs grew more tired, seemed to get steeper and steeper. I could stop occasionally investigating the noises in the woods that had caused unease when it was still dark.

As I hiked, I wondered, "When will I start to see rocks?" Up until then, it had been mostly dirt, hills, and trees. It didn't feel like I was on a mountain yet. Soon, though, the terrain began to change. Nearing the top of a hill, the trail made a turn, and small bits of rock began to poke through the dirt. As I rounded the bend, larger rocks emerged, then boulders. The trail gradually transformed from a gentle forest hike into the rugged, rocky mountain that had drawn me here years ago.

Eventually, the trail became a rocky staircase. To my left, offshoot paths climbed a short incline, a perfect spot to take a break and enjoy the view. I made the little jog up, and to my surprise, it led to a ridgeline with incredible sights. The drop-off in front of me revealed the vast Mount Thielsen wilderness, part of the Umpqua National Forest: hills and trees stretched as far as I could see. To my left, Diamond Lake sparkled. To my right, the steep southern slope of the mountain revealed years of broken basaltic andesite rock, shaped by glaciers in the winter and pounded by summer thunderstorms.

While I was taking it all in, I noticed a tent set up along the ridgeline. Up until that point, I hadn't seen anyone else on the hike. I hadn't been expecting to, given my early start, but seeing that someone else was also out there gave me a quiet sense of connection. Sometimes, knowing someone else is pursuing their path reminds us that we're not alone in climbing our own mountains.

Once I reached the ridgeline, the mountain finally revealed itself in full. The rocky terrain was unlike anything I had seen on previous hikes. The way the rocks jutted upward, pushing against the mountain, gave the peak a jagged, almost alien appearance. Spires of stone stretched toward the sky, casting sharp shadows and forming shapes that seemed sculpted by some otherworldly hand. For a moment, it felt less like a mountain in Oregon and more like an entirely different planet. I couldn't stop staring, taking in the stark, raw beauty of the landscape, realizing this was the terrain I had dreamed about for years.

As I navigated the rocky switchbacks, I became more aware of my body and how it interacted with the trail. My hands instinctively checked my pack, making sure the waist straps were snug to transfer weight from my shoulders to my hips. Each step required attention, finding a stable footing, planting my feet carefully, and keeping a steady rhythm. The air near the top was crisp and fresh, filling my lungs and energizing me with every breath. Despite the soreness in my legs, my careful adjustments and awareness helped me feel in control and capable.

Mentally, I felt surprisingly calm. I had played this moment in my mind countless times, preparing for the point when I would need to slow down, think through each step, and navigate the increasingly rocky trail. Now that I was here, those mental rehearsals paid off. My thoughts stayed focused, even as excitement bubbled beneath the surface. Each glance at the approaching summit reminded me of how far I'd come, through preparation, smaller hikes, and the perseverance to overcome previous setbacks. Reflection and exhilaration mingled as I realized I was truly about to accomplish the goal I had set years ago.

As I continued along the ridgeline, the trees thinned. Eventually, I emerged fully from the forest and faced the towering mountain ahead. The short, steep switchbacks demanded frequent breaks to catch my breath and sip water. But the progress was undeniable. I was seeing the terrain I had imagined for years, the same rocky slopes that first sparked the goal of hiking Mount Thielsen.

Our personal goals are often like this. If we stick with them long enough, we begin to see a clearer picture of where we started, where we are, and where we want to go. Reflection matters. Looking back on the progress we've made can reignite motivation to keep moving forward.

I think of my Spanish practice as an example. Progress has been slow, and at times it feels like I'm hardly improving. But small moments, such as communicating with a goat herder near our property or working with a player on my son's soccer team who doesn't speak English, remind me that I have grown. Even limited ability can lead to meaningful interactions, and those glimpses of success are what push me to keep going.

The same goes for other goals. My wife recently returned to school, and before she started, she questioned whether the timing was right. The costs, the adjustments, the reliance on friends and family, it all started to seem too much. But once school finally started, it didn't take more than a few days of going, and that excitement took over. Beginning that trail and seeing progress, even small steps toward her goal in just a couple of days, she found that momentum and reassurance that this is what she wanted. The trials and challenges that came with it would be worth it in the end, when she accomplished her goal and completed her school.

Momentum is a tricky thing. Sometimes, reaching a midpoint in a goal, when you can even glimpse the end, doesn't make the journey easier. The trail gets steeper. Obstacles appear. The shade disappears. Fatigue sets in. But momentum compounds when we take deliberate, consistent steps.

I've noticed this while cycling. Longer rides have become possible as my legs have grown stronger, and I've learned better nutrition for energy. But longer rides also come with new challenges: more water to carry, discomfort on the seat, or a flat tire far from home. The journey continues to test me, even as I build strength and skill.

In the same way, staying mindful of the bigger picture helps. Look back at the distance you've covered. Look around at where you are. Look ahead at how far you still have to go. Each glance gives a small boost of confidence to keep moving forward. Step by step. One switchback at a time.

Progress also comes from intentional tools and practices. Just like packing gear for a challenging hike, we can "pack" for life goals. Daily habits, apps, accountability partners, or the right resources can all keep us moving. But tools only work if they serve the purpose; they can't replace clarity or commitment. A streak in an app is motivating, but without remembering why you started, it's hollow. A bike ride teaches endurance, but only if you push through the discomfort and pay attention to incremental improvement.

The ridgeline reminded me of this principle. From the forest floor to the rocky slope, each small gain brought a new view and renewed motivation. Each careful step was preparation and progress at once. And sometimes, you only notice the progress you've made when you pause, take a breath, and look around. That moment of perspective is often what fuels the next push forward.

By the time I reached the steeper switchbacks, I was seeing what I had hoped for: the mountain, the valleys, the lake below, and the terrain that had first drawn me in. These glimpses were not just about scenery; they were reminders that persistence matters. Those small steps add up. The preparation, momentum, and reflection can carry you through challenges.

In the end, the trail, like our goals, is climbed one step at a time. Some steps are easy, some are grueling. Some reveal breathtaking views, while others remind us of the distance still ahead. But as long as we keep our eyes on what we're building toward, the progress we've made, and the tools we've packed along the way, we keep moving forward. Step by step. One switchback at a time.

CHAPTER 5

RISING HIGHER, THE REWARD OF PERSISTENCE

As I continued up the small but steep switchbacks, I found myself stopping more and more often. The incline was getting to me, no doubt about it. And, I'm sure the elevation wasn't doing me any favors either; I was hovering around 9,000 feet now, where every breath seemed thinner, every step heavier. Each pause gave me a moment to collect myself, to let my lungs catch up to my legs. When I looked up, I could see the end of the trail inching closer with each effort, like a prize dangling just out of reach but not beyond possibility.

Eventually, the trail itself began to fade. The familiar dirt path and loose gravel were behind me, and in their place stood rock. At that point, I wasn't just hiking anymore; I was bear-crawling up the jagged face of the peak that had drawn me here in the first place.

This was where all those intimidating words I had read beforehand: technical, scramble, spire, exposure, suddenly became real. Every movement had to be deliberate. Every handhold, every step required thought and care. There was no margin for error here. No trees to catch me. No railings to lean on. No one else to spot me. I was exposed, completely vulnerable, and completely alone.

I pressed forward anyway. Inch by inch. Breath by breath. My legs screamed in protest with each push upward. Five miles of steady climbing had already drained much of my strength, but I willed myself onward. This was the final stretch.

Finally, I came across a natural seat in the rocks, almost looking like it was carved out for weary climbers like me. I slipped my backpack off and set it carefully on a small ledge beside me, then lowered myself down to rest. For the first time in hours, I wasn't pushing forward; I was just sitting, breathing, and observing.

As I settled into that natural seat, I took a moment to simply breathe and look around. My body, though having climbed thousands of feet, felt surprisingly relaxed. The fatigue that had weighed on my legs for hours seemed to melt away, replaced by awe and gratitude. I noticed the birds circling high above, gliding effortlessly on the wind. Their presence was calming, a reminder that life continues in its rhythm even at the highest points. A slight breeze brushed my face, refreshing and cooling against the warmth of the sun, whose rays had finally broken free from the morning haze. In that moment, it hit me: we are capable of more than we often realize. Hard things can be done. Goals can be achieved. Clarity comes when we rise above the familiar, step by step.

And what a view it was.

From that perch, I could see the mountain in a way I never had before. The spire loomed directly in front of me, sharp and commanding, but just as striking were the countless other spires jutting up from the rock around me. It was like standing in a cathedral not made by human hands.

Being alone at the end of the trail brought a unique perspective. There was no one to distract me, no chatter, no immediate company to share my thoughts with. Instead, I was left with only myself, the mountain, and the horizon stretching for miles. It was intimate, personal, and almost sacred. I could reflect on the journey—the preparation, the setbacks, the unexpected storms, and even the years I had spent waiting for this moment. Facing the climb solo reinforced that accomplishment isn't just about the destination or the view; it's about proving to yourself that you can endure, adapt, and rise above challenges without relying on anyone else.

I studied the terrain, realizing just how unique it truly was. The massive plates of earth that had pushed upward against this ancient volcanic core had created something extraordinary. The mountain's surface was bare, stark, and unfamiliar, unlike any other mountain I had hiked before. No lush forests, no soft alpine meadows, just rock, raw, harsh and unapologetic.

From my seat, I could trace my entire journey. Off in the distance lay the road I had driven in on, the very place where I first glimpsed this peak years ago. There was the lake I had camped at the night before. I could see the blackened scar of the forest fire I had hiked through in the dark that morning. My eyes followed the ridgeline where I had crossed paths with the other hiker packing up his tent. I could even make out the trail winding up from the tree line, turning into the steep switchbacks that had brought me to the rocks where I now sat.

As I sat there, I soaked in the details of the rocky spire and the surrounding peaks. The jagged edges, the stubborn patches of greenery clinging to cracks in the stone, and the sheer drop-offs reminded me that even the harshest terrain has its life, its resilience, and its beauty. The mountain was teaching me silently: preparation, persistence, and respect for the process matter. Just as the rocks had endured time, wind, and weather to form something remarkable, we too must face challenges, adapt, and shouldn't give up in the face of hardships, and when we start doing so, we begin taking our steps toward our growth and reaching our own peaks.

And it wasn't just the big picture that caught my eye; it was the details. Patches of bushes, already changing into their fall colors, splashes of gold and red against the grey stone. Tiny, green plants, clinging stubbornly to cracks where most life would wither. Black crows circling high above, one of the few animals suited to these heights. I noticed a carved-out hollow in the rock where winter's glacier had slowly eaten its way into the mountain, leaving behind scars of ice and time.

The sun's rays warming my face added a layer of peace to the moment. Light has a way of highlighting not just the scenery, but our own journey. I thought about every step I had taken, from the early darkness, through the switchbacks, across the ridgeline, and finally to this rocky seat. Each step built on the last; each choice mattered. I realized that reaching a goal isn't a single moment but a collection of decisions, efforts, and reflections that carry us forward. And right here, right now, the combination of effort, patience, and resilience created something profound: clarity, pride, and an unshakable sense of accomplishment.

And then it hit me: I had done it. I hiked Mount Thielsen.

For a moment, though, disappointment crept in. I wasn't at the very tip-top. To get there would have required actual climbing, straight up the spire, possibly with ropes and gear, depending on how brave you were—not just scrambling. I was so close, and part of me ached to touch that highest point.

But reality sobered me quickly. I was a mile away from the nearest hiker. Five to six miles from the trailhead. Hours from any help should I fall. And I was exhausted, completely spent from the long, steep push to get here. Maybe on another day, with a partner and the right gear, I could have attempted it. But not today.

At first, that realization stung. I had come this far, only to stop just shy of the ultimate summit. But then I remembered my original goal: to hike Mount Thielsen. And sitting there, I realized, 'That's exactly what I had done. I had prepared, pushed, persisted, and made it.' My goal was accomplished.

The top of the spire could wait for another day. For now, I was satisfied… even more than satisfied. I was proud.

I lingered there, letting the joy sink in. I took pictures, not just to capture the view but to remind myself of the feeling. And then, to my surprise, I discovered I had cell service. On a whim, I called Tiffany. Her face lit up on the screen as I panned the camera around, showing her the rugged beauty that surrounded me. She had been cheering me on from the start of this adventure, and even though she wasn't physically beside me, at that moment, I could share my victory with her.

There is something powerful about having others witness your accomplishments. The people who encourage you along the way make the summit all the sweeter.

As I sat there, I remembered a story I once read about a mountain guide. He led hikers along a winding trail that dipped into valleys, crossed rivers, and climbed ridges before eventually reaching the summit. One hiker asked him why they didn't just take the direct route straight up. The guide answered that without the valleys, without the rivers, without the longer path, the summit wouldn't feel the same. The journey gives meaning to the destination.

That truth came alive for me on this mountain. The early morning darkness, the burn scar, the switchbacks and the exhaustion; all of it made this moment richer. The joy wasn't just in arriving—it was in knowing what it took to get there.

There's a reason our bodies reward us when we accomplish something difficult. Science tells us that completing a goal releases dopamine, a chemical that fills us with joy, confidence, and motivation to keep going. I believe that's by divine design. Our Creator didn't just make us capable of growth; He wired us to want to grow, to find joy in progress, to keep reaching higher.

And yet, sometimes I feel almost embarrassed writing about this climb. After all, Mount Thielsen isn't Everest. It's not even the tallest peak in Oregon. There are people out there summiting far greater challenges, both on mountains and in life. But here's what I've come to realize: comparison steals the joy of accomplishment.

We all have different goals, different strengths, and different seasons of life. For some, Everest is the goal. For others, it's Thielsen. For others still, it might be something that seems small on the outside but monumental on the inside, like reading four books in a year when you've barely read four in the past decade.

What matters isn't how your goal compares to someone else's. What matters is that it stretches you. That it pushes you beyond your comfort zone into growth.

Growth happens when we're willing to push ourselves beyond what's comfortable. I've seen this truth play out not only in my own life but in my son Braxton's as well. One soccer season, because there weren't enough boys his age, he had to play in a group two age divisions above his own. Most of the boys were bigger, faster, stronger, and far more experienced. At first, it was intimidating—he had to fight just to keep up. But that challenge forced him to stretch in ways he never would have otherwise. He learned new techniques, developed sharper instincts, and grew in confidence with every game. Before long, he was starting regularly and playing most of each match. What began as an uncomfortable push turned into one of his greatest seasons of growth—physically, mentally, and even emotionally.

That experience reminded me that growth rarely comes in the easy seasons. It happens when we're stretched, challenged, and placed just beyond what feels possible—when we're willing to step into the uphill, the unfamiliar, or the intimidating. That's where progress lives.

Because in the end, the end of the trail isn't just a place; it's a feeling. It's the reward of persistence. It's that deep, unshakable joy of knowing: I did it. I kept going. I rose higher than I thought I could.

And that's a feeling worth chasing again and again.

As I sat there one last time, the wind brushing against the rocks around me, I knew it was time to start my way back down. The climb had pushed me, tested me, and rewarded me. But as every hiker knows, the journey isn't complete until you return to where you began. The mountain had taught me its lessons on the way.

CHAPTER 6

DESCENDING THE MOUNTAIN; SEEING WITH NEW EYES

I took off my sweatshirt and put it in my backpack. It was cooler on top of the mountain, especially with the elevation I was at. But the sun was up in the sky by now, bringing warmth. The first little while of navigating down the rocks was a challenge. As I mentioned before, there really was no trail at this point, just rock. That meant I had to find the best path down that I could, something that wouldn't hurt me too badly.

Every now and then, I'd slip on a loose section. I kept myself low to the ground to maintain balance. I probably looked ridiculous. I could hear groups of hikers as their talks echoed off the rocks. They were still back in the tree line, and I couldn't see them yet. I remembered being there earlier, looking up to where I now was, and thinking about how silly I must have looked trying to navigate this terrain. But I also knew they would understand the challenges soon enough.

I finally got off the steep rocks, back to the loose gravel. The switchbacks that were clear on the way up were not so obvious on the way down. From above, the lines that once guided me seemed blurred. More than once, I stopped, looking down, trying to find the path. At times, I couldn't see it at all, so I had to focus on where I knew I came from and travel in that direction.

Eventually, I made it back to the ridgeline. The trail became much more defined, and my pace quickened. I ran into about four different small groups of people on the way down. Each asked how far I had made it, how it was going, and most of them mentioned they hoped to beat the afternoon storm that had been forecast.

I encouraged them to keep going. Told them how amazing the view was near the top. I wanted to be that supporter, keeping others motivated to reach their goal. And as I spoke, I realized that encouragement itself was a kind of reward, like sharing a glimpse of the end's perspective, not just the climb.

The journey down offered an entirely different perspective. I wasn't focused on the steep climb or reaching the top; I had already accomplished that. Now I could notice the scenery. I saw the deep green of the forest, the wildflowers pushing up through the burn scar, proof that even after hardship, growth continues. Even the forest has its own resilience.

In daylight, the scenery was even more rewarding. The clarity allowed me to see details I had only imagined during the dark ascent. I could hear the birds better and found myself stopping to watch them, trying to identify each one. The forest seemed alive in a new way; the wind rustling through the pines, the sun glinting off leaves, and the chirps and calls of animals. It felt like a type of reward, a visual and auditory gift for completing the climb.

I stopped occasionally to watch woodpeckers searching for bugs in the bark, blue jays hunting for nuts in the pines, and the occasional chipmunk scurrying across the trail. At one point, a squirrel dropped something from a tree. When he came back to pick it up, I realized it was a pinecone almost as big as he was. Simple moments like that reminded me to pay attention, to notice life in all its quiet persistence.

As I continued downward, I started to feel the fatigue I hadn't noticed at the summit. My feet were sore, my legs ached from the downhill strain, and hunger began to set in. I was on my last protein bar, and thoughts of the peanut butter and jelly sandwiches waiting in the truck made my stomach growl. These small physical reminders grounded me, showing that even after success, the body needs care and attention.

As I neared the end of the hike, some of the forest felt familiar, even though I had only glimpsed it in the darkness at the start. Now, in full daylight, everything appeared clearer. The trailhead came into view, along with information boards I had missed earlier. One noted that in 1964, Congress had established this as a Wilderness Area to protect and maintain its "wild character." In a small way, I felt a part of that wild character, having traversed and respected it, becoming a small witness to its continued life.

The sense of direction after completing the climb was full of joy. On my way back down, I found myself asking: "Now what?" Now that I had achieved this goal, one I had worked toward for years, what was next? Should I find a bigger mountain? Steeper? Longer? I didn't have an answer yet, but completing this hike had awakened a desire to continue seeking new challenges and new heights.

Reaching the end of the trail left me certain I could set new goals and achieve them, as long as I put in the preparation and kept pushing forward. The climb had proven something important: persistence, preparation, and focus could carry me to heights I had long envisioned. The mountain became a metaphor for every goal I would pursue next.

Often, accomplishing goals starts habits in motion. My Spanish goal created the habit of daily practice. My goal of reading four books in a year encouraged me to read more consistently. I still don't read as much as I'd like, but I read far more than I ever did before. Once we push through the beginning stage, focusing consistently on our goal, our bodies and minds sync up with our efforts. The work begins to feel instinctive, part of a larger rhythm.

Some goals, especially spiritual or intellectual ones, are similar. They often don't have a clear finish line, yet progress comes line upon line, precept upon precept. Small, consistent steps build over time. Each effort may feel insignificant on its own, but gradually they combine into something greater, a perspective and growth that you realize only by looking back. Just like the mountain, the lessons aren't always obvious in the moment; they unfold quietly as we move forward.

This hike was a goal with a clear finish line, but many goals are less tangible. Learning a language, for instance, rarely has a sharp endpoint. Even if fluency is the goal, learning never truly stops. Intellectual and spiritual goals, in particular, often have no absolute end, only continued ascent. Each new understanding encourages another; each insight fuels curiosity and growth.

Goals that we set intellectually or spiritually, even, I feel, rarely have a clear-cut end to them. But rather a lot of goals in those aspects have more of a continued progression that comes from them. An increased understanding of things leads us to wanting to learn the next thing or learn more.

Along the way, we may meet others still working toward the goals we've completed. It's important to offer encouragement. Remember the mental battles you faced, the doubts, the challenges, and extend a hand or a word to those climbing their own mountains. That shared humanity can make the journey lighter for everyone.

As I finished the hike, I realized something crucial: the mountain had been my goal, but the journey was the lesson. The climb taught me patience, persistence, and presence. The descent revealed the beauty I had missed in pursuit of the peak. The people I met reminded me of the value of encouragement and shared effort. The forest, with its resilience and quiet life, offered a subtle spiritual lesson: growth comes in many forms, and even after hardship, life persists.

Reaching the end of the trail, I felt the satisfaction of completion, but also the quiet stirring of something ongoing. Goals, whether tangible (like this hike), intellectual (like learning), or spiritual, may have different endpoints, but the journey shapes us in ways the destination alone cannot. Rising higher, both literally and metaphorically, is less about standing on the summit and more about the steady climb, the habits formed, the lessons learned, and the perspective gained.

The mountain was my goal. The journey, in every sense, was the lesson.

EPILOGUE

Beyond The Summit

When I think back on the climb, I can still feel the texture of the rocks beneath my hands, the burn in my legs with every switchback, and the steady rhythm of my breath against the silence of the mountain. Reaching the summit was a moment of awe and gratitude, but I've come to realize that the actual reward wasn't only at the top; it lived in the journey itself—the careful steps, the moments of patience, and the quiet awareness of God's creations all around me. The woodpeckers, the chipmunks, the wildflowers reclaiming a burned patch of forest, all whispered a truth our Heavenly Father seems to teach again and again: growth happens gradually, step by step, line upon line, precept upon precept.

That truth feels especially clear when I think about spiritual goals. Unlike a mountain peak, faith has no finish line. You don't "complete" your relationship with God or your understanding of Christ's teachings. Instead, it's a continual climb. Some days feel slow, even repetitive, but each small effort builds on the last. Whether it's prayer, study, service, or quiet reflection, those consistent acts shape who we are becoming. The Lord sees every faithful step, even the ones that feel unseen or uncertain.

There were moments on the trail when the path was unclear or the loose gravel shifted underfoot. In those moments, I had to trust myself, the preparation I had done, and the quiet assurance that I could find my footing again. Spiritually, I've felt that same uncertainty at times when answers didn't come quickly or when progress felt invisible. Yet, just like on the mountain, persistence mattered more than perfection. Our Heavenly Father asks us to keep moving, to trust in the lessons we've already learned, and to believe that He walks beside us even when the way forward isn't clear.

Looking back, I see that the journey itself changed me more than the summit ever could. Accomplishment has its joy, but growth happens in the process, through the habits we form, the patience we practice, the humility we learn. On the descent, I noticed details I had missed on the way up: the soft light through the trees, the quiet beauty of the forest waking in the morning. That shift in awareness mirrored what reflection does in life. Perspectives allow us to see where we've been and recognize how far we've come. The climb builds strength; the reflection builds understanding.

Encouragement became one of the sweetest parts of that descent. Meeting others still climbing, and offering a word of support, reminded me that our personal growth isn't meant to stay personal. Our Heavenly Father blesses us not just to bless ourselves but to lift others. Sharing what we've learned, giving guidance, or simply offering empathy allows our progress to ripple outward. Just as I had benefited from those who came before me on the trail, others can find confidence in the paths we've already walked.

One lesson that continues to guide me is that lasting growth is built through small, deliberate steps. Habits become characters. Daily efforts, whether in prayer, learning, service, or study, create the quiet rhythm of discipleship. My Spanish practice, my reading goal, and now this book all grew from that same principle: steady, humble effort brings transformation. It's less about the moment you "arrive" and more about who you are becoming along the way. Even when the steps feel repetitive or invisible, each builds toward something greater, just as the mountain taught me through every careful move upward.

As I walked back through the forest, I realized how deeply this hike reflected the pattern of life itself. The climb represents effort and discipline; the summit, fulfillment and gratitude; the descent, reflection and renewed vision. Each part matters. We are not meant to stay at the top, but to carry out the perspective gained there into what comes next. In that sense, each goal, whether physical, intellectual, or spiritual, is both an ending and a beginning. The strength we build in one season becomes the foundation for the next.

I was especially moved by the way the forest showed signs of renewal. Burned areas were now full of life, with black ground now covered with a bed of wildflowers. Fallen trees became nourishment for new growth. It reminded me that setbacks, challenges, and even failures can be part of God's refining process. His plan allows for renewal. Just as the forest thrives after fire, we too can heal and grow stronger through adversity when we trust His timing and grace.

Reaching the trailhead again, seeing where it all began, I felt a deep sense of peace. There was joy in finishing, yes, but also gratitude, for the process, the lessons, and the quiet assurance that growth continues. Our Heavenly Father's plan for us is not one summit but many, each offering perspective and preparation for the next. Life is a continual climb toward becoming more like Him, steadily, faithfully, joyfully.

The mountain is more than a metaphor. It's a reminder that progress is both physical and spiritual; that faith and effort intertwine. Christ Himself showed us that growth, endurance, and service are sacred forms of worship. When we follow that example, when we keep moving, learning, and reaching outward, we align ourselves with divine purpose.

So, as I walk away from the trailhead, I carry the mountain with me. Not as something finished, but as part of who I am now. Each goal, each habit, each act of faith becomes another step on an eternal path of learning and becoming. The summit is sweet, but the journey, the humble, persistent, faithful journey, is where joy is found.

Thank you for taking the time to walk this trail with me through these pages. Just as the climb taught me to move deliberately, to notice the small wonders along the way, and to trust each step even when the path was unclear, I hope these reflections encourage you in your own journey. Whether your goal is just beginning or you are persevering through a difficult stretch, you may find joy in the process, patience in the challenges, and awareness in the quiet moments. Remember that growth, like the forest recovering after a fire, happens gradually, and that each small effort contributes to the person you are becoming. I hope that by reading this story, you feel inspired to start your own climb, to reflect on the lessons you gather along the way, and to trust in the guidance of our Heavenly Father as you continue toward your summits, both seen and unseen.